Because of the Customer

Seven Recipes
For
Success
In Business

Frank D. Briggs

A Gourmet's Guide to Customer Service

Order this book online at www.trafford.com
or email orders@trafford.com

Most Trafford titles are also available at major online book retailers.

Printed in the United States of America.

ISBN: 978-1-4269-2642-6 (sc)
ISBN: 978-1-4269-2643-3 (hc)
ISBN: 978-1-4269-7842-5 (e)

Library of Congress Control Number: 2010901220

Trafford rev. 08/14/2012

Trafford PUBLISHING® www.trafford.com

North America & international
toll-free: 1 888 232 4444 (USA & Canada)
phone: 250 383 6864 ♦ fax: 812 355 4082

To my family: my wife Ruth, my daughter Blythe
and my son Austin for their endless love and support:
who stood behind me, believed in me when I struggled to
continue writing and encouraged me through all of my
disparity. And also, Don Morgan: Friend, mentor & fellow
Toastmaster, who inspired me to reach inside myself and find
the greatness within.

"The true measure of your life is not how well you live, but how well others live because of you."

Bill Gates

Introduction
by: Blythe Briggs

Dawning that fateful day when ancient man discovered fire he has striven to create ways to make life easier. From the wheel to the TV dinner we have tried to simplify and refine the way we live. With the creative nature of man also came the spirit of man to compete for dominance in the market place, thus customer service was born.

Ever since man has created products different from his merchant brothers and inter-market competition spawned there has been a need to make individual businesses stand out. At first it was in the quality of products alone, the best wool merchant got the gold, but soon: other wool merchants had the same products. Now, this same wool merchant had to come up with new ways to keep his customers. He had to win them over: with better prices, better deals: better customer service.

As consumers, we too are often confronted with a barrage of choices: it's like walking into the perfume section of a department store. As you get closer to those pretty boxes and carefully done up displays, the many scents of perfume beguile you, confusing you, which one has the sweetest scent, which one will take his breath away? Suddenly you walk up to the counter wanting more of that beautiful smell that drew you in.

But: What causes you to buy it? Is it that beautiful smell, the pretty package or is it like most that live up to its name? Maybe with this perfume my thighs will shrink, my breasts will grow, and the man of my dreams, like the one from the commercials will knock on my door carry me away on the back of a beautiful white stallion. The truth is that none of these things influence your decision. It is much simpler then that. You look at the price, talk with the sales person behind the counter, and if they convince you that the most expensive perfume is right for you and wins you over with customer service, you may buy it.

Our busy market place is like the perfume section and too often we forget that beyond the advertising, the pretty bottles, we are all trying to peddle the same scented water. How do we do it? By winning over the hearts of our customers: with better customer service.

So wouldn't it help us all out, if we customer service professionals stopped thinking of quarterly profits: pie charts and grafts and started thinking first a little more about what really matters: The customers, and customer service.

Foreword
by: Austin Briggs

My dad was always a project orientated kind of guy. Some
of my earliest memories were when my parents bought our
first house. This 900 sq. ft. home on 4th Ave. even in the most
appreciative of light was at best a "fixer-upper". At the age of
three, I can in the vaguest sense remember my dad leading the
charge of project after project spending days, weeks, months
and years transforming that little shack from an eyesore of a
home that to the average person had no chance of ever looking
like a home again, to one that would get long time neighbors
to stop and take a look. Some of these things like painting and
landscaping took place in a short period of time (exact numbers
are escaping me, probably due to my age at the time) before we
moved in, and the rest was done in the five years we lived there.

After five years in our little house on 4th Ave. we ventured
to move again, to a newer home with more space on 18th
street just a mile away from our first home. Again my father

set out to improve our humble abode, from a simple project of removing an old worn out fountain and pond in favor of more green grass for the family dog, to the complex and back-breaking task as seen in his adventure to (successfully) build a 10 x 12 ft. garden shed from scratch with no plans to redoing a large patio area and countless other projects in and around our home. We have moved twice since then, but I will spare you the summarized versions of my fathers exploits in home-improvements to restate simply what I have previously said.

My father is, was, and as far as I can tell will always be a project orientated man.

I tell you this not to captivate you with stories of my father building picture frames for the countless memories he managed to save, and certainly not to talk to you about my dad's seemingly natural aptitude for doing a job right and finishing it early, for these things would have no place in the front of this book. I tell you this: rather, because I want you to see my dad in the same light as I see him before you read his book and take in his knowledge. I want you to understand that this book is perhaps one of the most important projects I have ever seen my dad undertake.

This book is a culmination of my father's knowledge, passion, and first hand experience in the field of customer service. This book is very simply a piece of my fathers life, and a project he may never completely finish.

Preface

For over forty years now I have worked with customers. Ever since I was a young man twelve years of age I have been involved in customer service jobs.

My very first job was that of a paperboy in rural Pierce County Washington with a bike as my transportation. I have been a salesman, food service worker, truck driver, delivery person and have had many similar jobs where I have been on the forefront of customer service. One thing that I have learned is that without customers I would not have a job. But most important, without customer service there would be **NO** customers.

How many times have you as a customer been treated poorly? You know what I am talking about. Slow service, little or no choices, treated like an idiot. Now I could go on and on, but I know by now that you are already forming your own list of poor customer service situations that you have encountered, RIGHT! I thought so! You are not alone.

Sadly enough all too many times we pass those same poor customer service traits on to our own customers, and then wonder why we are losing business.

I have put this book together to show you just how easy it is to succeed, or fail when you lose sight of the most fundamental aspects of business: Customer service.

When it comes to customer service it does not matter what your job is or; the hierarchy of the company where you work. Everybody, I mean everybody plays a crucial role in the success of a company's future. From the Janitor to the CEO, along with everyone in between uses customer service to do their job. It is crucial to remember that we must do our job like the future depends on it, and that everything we have or could ever want is all based on our ability to offer quality customer service.

Think of the customer first each and every time. Treat the customer the way that you would like to be treated, and your success will flourish, all...

Because of the Customer

Acknowledgement

I wish to thank the Selling North Idaho Toastmasters (SNIT) group for their support and feedback in the early stages of my project when it was just a speech. I would also like to Thank Steven K. Scott, Ken Blanchard and the late Frank Bettger. These authors and their inspiring writings which helped show me how to put my words into this book, they too gave me the confidence and courage to continue writing even when I wanted to put it all aside. And finally I would like to acknowledge all those who have walked the path of customer service before me who believe, like myself that without customer service we would have no customers. Without customers we would have nothing.

Table of Contents

Because of the customer;
I have a headache.

Because of the Customer;
I missed my lunch.

Because of the Customer;
I had to postpone my vacation.

Because of the Customer;
I just got promoted.

Because of the Customer;
I just put a down payment on my new home.

Because of the Customer;
I was able to take my dream vacation.

They say for every action, there is an equal
and opposite re-action.

Customer service is really no different, for every time
we are rude and nasty to a customer it affects our financial
standing. In most cases it has a direct affect on our customers
willingness to do repeat business with us, or
for that fact the kind of reference we will receive.

Think of it simply as this, as you walk down a street, a hallway
or even the local mall or shopping center; watch people as
you smile and say hello, almost every time you will get back a
warm response. But, try being a little rude
and see just how much more of a response you will get.

As you read ahead you will see through the experiences
of Jamie, Eric, Mr. Smith & Thadeus Sternhaven the
differences between good and bad customer service, along
with customer service situations that I have encountered.
Through these examples you will see just how easy customer
service can be when you think of the customers needs first
before your own needs and wants.
Through these experiences I hope this will help you realize
that everything you have or could ever want is all.

Because of the Customer

Chapter I.

<u>Because the Customer has a need.</u>

"Why are we in business?"
Mr. Smith

Graduation day June 2000 Rileyville College would be the stepping off point for two very different graduates.

Eric was the Captain of the football team, class valedictorian who finished top of his class. Eric was an out-spoken business major: short tempered, arrogant and very competitive. Eric did not believe in volunteering for anything, he always stood alone and never trusted anyone.

For Eric it was always about me, me, me, if it did not benefit him he would not do it. Eric's reputation proceeded him; whether he was playing football, doing class projects or anything else, it was all about Eric. Eric was also known to take any shortcuts possible: Eric would lie or cheat, any means he could find just to accomplish his goals.

After graduation, Eric landed a job with Sternhaven Incorporated International (Stinc Int'l) as an up and coming sales executive. Sternhaven Incorporated had offices in five major cities in four countries around the world.
Eric was given a nice office, a luxury car and a very generous six figure expense account. Mr. Sternhaven: the president of the company, took an instant shine to his new protégé. Eric's resume was so impressive that when Mr. Sternhaven read it he knew he had made the right choice, and was assured that he would not be disappointed.

Then there was Jamie, an average student; a soft spoken business major who had to work extra hard just to succeed. Jamie was somewhat shy when it came to group discussions, but she had a heart of gold and always tried to find the very best in every situation. Jamie like to volunteer for several different charities, she liked the teamwork that it taught her and the sense of pride she felt when she accomplished difficult tasks while working closely with those around her. Jamie knew that she could not do these things by herself, but needed others working with her. Ask anyone who knew Jamie and they will tell you that she would go out of her way to help those in need.

After graduation Jamie landed herself a job working at Smith's Apparel Wholesalers as a sales rep. The company was located in the heart of a depressed part of the city in a small rundown building; and Jamie still drove the used car her parents gave her after graduating high school. Now Mr. Smith could not offer Jamie a fancy office, or a large expense account. All Mr. Smith could offer her was a simple desk in the back corner of an over-crowded office and a starting wage of $25,000.00. Above her desk there was a sign for everyone to read which stated: **Because of the Customer.**

Thadeus Sternhaven graduated from college in 1965, he was class President, Captain of the debate team and Valedictorian. Orphaned in 1956 Thadeus had a difficult time finishing school, he had been bounced from home to home each time learning that success only comes from those who work hard to earn it. Thadeus had worked himself through college doing whatever he could to earn money; and with each dime he earned he quickly put it aside, but he also never forgot those who had helped him along the way: teaching him kindness and humility.

While attending college Thadeus Sternhaven not only gained an education from school; but also from his boss and mentor on the power of customer service. Thadeus had quickly learned from his job at the Trading Company that he should treat customers the way that he would want to be treated. After graduation, Thadeus took the money he had earned through college and in the fall of 1965 became a partner in business at The Trading Company

Thadeus quickly gained success as a partner of the Trading Company and within a year they had seven new employee's working in a small overcrowded office. Success continued over the next two years as Thadeus became more and more powerful in the marketplace and as a driving force for the success of The Trading Company; but changes were soon to come, changes that would change Thadeus. The Trading Company had grown so much because of Thadeus Sternhaven's hard work; he had become troubled by his partner's willingness to ignore his recommendations that they needed more space, so. In 1969 Thadeus Sternhaven bought his partner's share of the business, relocated the Trading Company to a larger building and changed the company's name to Sternhaven Incorporated.

As his success grew over the next decade so did the need for more and more office space, he now had 10,000 employee's working in four different cities nationwide.
By 1980 Mr. Sternhaven's empire had grown so much that he opened his first office overseas, renaming his company to Sternhaven Incorporated International (Stinc Int'l).

Christopher Smith flunked out of high school in 1980, he found whatever work he could to earn money.
Christopher always had a way with people, and went out of his way to make customers happy. This typically resulted in very handsome tips which he earnestly saved. Christopher had a banner year in 1992 when Mr. Anderson, a local business owner, seeing Christopher's customer service prowess hired him as his new assistant manager.
While working twelve hour days seven days a week, Christopher also attended night school where he received not only his GED, but also a minor degree in business.

Christopher Smith was the kind of employee that every employer would like to have, knowing the importance of teamwork he would regularly jump in to help others get their work done, encouraging them by his leadership. Christopher knew the importance of customer service through teamwork, and had come up with a list of seven rules or recipes as he liked to call them that he had passed around to all of his fellow workers to use on a daily bases.

Mr. Anderson, Christopher's boss died suddenly in 1998 leaving the company vulnerable to bank foreclosure due to back debts. Facing his biggest challenge ever, Christopher quickly put together a plan to save the company based on the seven rules of customer service he practiced, along with a strategy of financial success. After a year of hard work and sacrifice Christopher Smith moved his fledgling company to a small run down overcrowded office, and in 1999 proudly changed the signage on the building from The Trading Company: to Smith's Apparel Wholesalers.

Now even though Mr. Sternhaven and Mr. Smith came from both ends of the business spectrum, one thing both men had in common: both held weekly meetings with their sales staff; for Mr. Smith, it was a cup of coffee at a small table in the break room: but not for Mr. Sternhaven.

Mr. Sternhaven had a large conference room with video hook-ups to his other offices around the world. His talks were always fierce and direct.
"I want you to **SELL! SELL! SELL!**"
He would tell his sales staff pounding his fist on the table, "Put the fear into your customers, that the only company for them is Sternhaven Incorporated International"

Eric was so impressed by Mr. Sternhavens dynamic, demanding nature. Eric often visualized himself vaulted to the position of company president someday; and so Eric asked Mr. Sternhaven for private sit down meetings in his office on a weekly basis.

"Of course my boy", Mr. Sternhaven told Eric, "I see great things from you in the future. Do everything I tell you and you cannot go wrong, First and foremost Eric my boy" Mr. Sternhaven continued, "Is to **SELL!, SELL!, SELL!**, Get that contract signed no matter what the cost, the bigger the better I always say. And do not worry if they can pay or not. Once we have a signed agreement, if they refuse to pay we'll let our corporate attorneys handle it"

Meanwhile over at Smith's Apparel Wholesalers, Mr. Smith and Jamie sat down for their first meeting over a cup coffee in a small break room at the back of their over-crowded office. On the wall just above the bulletin board Jamie noticed once again a banner that read:
Because of the Customer.

Jamie looked puzzled, she asked Mr. Smith.
"I noticed that are there two banners which read **Because of the Customer**, One in here and the other one that hangs over my desk in the main office, Why?"
"That's a great question Jamie" Mr. Smith replied.
"It's really a simple concept. No matter what we do, no matter what we have, everything is tied to those four simple words, **"Because of the Customer"**.

"Jamie" Mr. Smith said, "let me ask you a question, Why are we in business?"

Jamie thought for a moment: then replied timidly.
"Because we have something the customer needs"
"YES" Mr. Smith said. "Because we have something that the
customer needs: which brings me to my first rule Jamie.
Because the customer has a **NEED,**
We have a **JOB** to do."

Jamie smiled,
"I like that Mr. Smith," Jamie said "I have a job to do."

*   *   *

In today's tough market place we must walk carefully through
the fields of customer service. Making sure we do not step
in what those before us have left. With the latest technology,
today's customers are far more savvy than those of just a decade
ago. Customers today are not willing to put up with much B.S.
before they make a quick exit to safer pastures, and a customer
service person they can trust.

"BECAUSE THE CUSTOMER HAS A NEED, WE HAVE A JOB TO DO"

But, what kind of need does the customer have?

Informational, product or service?

For most businesses it is all three. Here, let me break it down
for you just a little bit more.

As I approached my fiftieth birthday I wanted a new digital
camera since I enjoy photography so much. I decided that I

would read up on all of the latest models with the features that I wanted. Not a small pocket size camera, but a full size SLR model for the more serious photographer. I talked with many people who had different brands and accessories, asked their opinions, what did they like or dislike about the one they had chose? After gathering enough information on various brands, reading publications on photography I was now ready to head out to the market place and start shopping for my new camera.

Six, That's the number of different stores I visited before I met Katy at a local electronics store. As I stood looking over the vast array of cameras before me; a short red-headed young lady stood across the rack of camera equipment from me and asked the most important first question.
"Would you like more information about any of the cameras you are looking at?" Katy inquired.
Information I thought to myself,
"Yes, as a matter of fact I would like more information" I said.
Katy then asked,
"What kind of photography will you be shooting? This will help me determine what camera will best suit your needs"

As I explained to her what kind of pictures I like to shoot, and those that I would like to learn how to shoot. I could see it in her eyes that she was gathering information and preparing her response to my questions.
Soon Katy had explained the benefits of the various models before me, and before long I had settled on the brand of camera that I had wanted from the start.
By taking the time to fully understand my needs, Katy had solidified my decision thru her helpful knowledge of the product along with her full understanding of my photographic needs.

When I finally made my purchase, I did not settle on the cheapest brand nor the most expensive model; in fact, I settled somewhere in the middle. When we take the time to listen, I mean really listen to our customers, as Katy did with me, we can break down some of the natural barriers the customers will put up as a defense mechanism to protect themselves from an over abrasive salesperson. Katy not only took the time to understand my needs, she took the time to explain the benefits of the products she was selling. Because of the knowledge Katy had, unlike the previous sales people I encountered, I felt more comfortable sharing more information with her, information that helped guide her in assisting me as I made my purchase.

Keep in mind that we have been given two ears and one mouth for a reason. This is so we can listen twice as much as we speak. By listening to our customers and fully understanding their needs we will help them rationalize their decision. How many times have we scared a potential customer away? Being too pushy, thinking of the sale or the potential commission first while ignoring the customers most basic needs. We all want to be successful in our sales and customers service; but we must remember that without customer service we have no customers, and without customers….well, you get the picture.
No matter what we do or sell, our customers first seek information about the product or service, and what benefit they will receive.

"Because the customer has a **NEED,**
we have a **JOB** to do."

Chapter II.

Because the customer has a choice.

"Let's refer to them as choices"
Mr. Smith

Now back over at Sternhaven Incorporated International, Mr. Sternhaven was having his weekly talk with his new young eager protégé`, Eric.
"Eric, my boy." Mr. Sternhaven said, between puffs on his cigar,
"It seems as if you have had a little trouble getting that first contract signed, correct"
"Yes sir," Eric replied.
"I have had a couple of meetings with clients, but nothing signed as of yet."
"Well what exactly do you tell them my boy?" Mr. Sternhaven inquired.

"Well sir, they tell me it's a nice deal…..but."
"BUT WHAT!" snapped Mr. Sternhaven.
"They tell me they want to see what our competition can offer."
Eric replied.
Mr. Sternhaven sat up in his chair, took two extra long puffs
off his cigar as he stared across the desk at Eric.
"Eric my boy, that's your problem, you are giving them a
choice" Mr. Sternhaven said. He continued,
"When you talk to your customers, you need to bad-mouth our
competition. Put some fear into them. Convince them that we
are the only company that can truly give them what they want."

"In my opinion Eric my boy," Mr. Sternhaven said.
"The customer has no choice; it is either Sternhaven or nobody".

*   *   *

"Good morning Mr. Smith" Jamie said politely.
"Good morning Jamie" Mr. Smith said. "How
was your weekend?"
"Ok" Jamie replied, "But I do have a question concerning
something a customer said to me last Friday"
"What is it?" Mr. Smith inquired.
Jamie took a sip of her coffee, gathered her thoughts and asked:
"How do you reply to customers when they mention our
competition?"
Mr. Smith smiled when he replied.
"First of all Jamie" he said. "I do not like the term competitor
used when I talk to customers, to me it sounds like we must
win at any cost. Forgetting what is most important to us, the
customer. Remember Jamie my first rule."

"Yes Mr. Smith" Jamie said.
"Because the customer has a Need, we have a Job to do."

"Well then Jamie," Mr. Smith continued. "Let us not refer to them as the competition to our customers, instead let us refer to them as choices, which brings me to my second rule."
"Because the customer has a **CHOICE,**
we must be the **BETTER** choice."

"Jamie" Mr. Smith asked. "Have you ever watched the original Miracle on 34th Street."
"OH YES! Mr. Smith: that is my all time favorite holiday movie. I just love little Natalie Wood: she really brought the character of Susan to life."
"Yes she did Jamie" Mr. Smith said. "But Jamie, do you remember what happened when the Macy's Santa sent a Macy's customer over to Gimbals?"
"Who could forget" Jamie replied. "Macy's realized that by creating a book showing what their competition had that they didn't, their customers could do the rest of the Holiday Shopping"
"AND?" Mr. Smith inquired.

Jamie thought for a moment and then blurted out.
"Macy's showed the customers that they had a choice, and in doing so became the better choice."
"Precisely Jamie" Mr. Smith said, "and remember: Because the customer has a choice, we must be the better choice. That is why Jamie we must always know what our competition is doing."

Drive down any business district street of a larger town or city and you will have many choices facing you. Fast food, gas stations, sit down restaurants, coffee shops, etc. etc. Choices, choices and more choices, But what makes us the better choice? Location, price, variety of products and services: or customer service? In reality it is all of the above. One attribute stands out above all the rest, customer service. That's right, customer service!

That is why our homework never stops, we must always know what our competition is doing. By listening to radio and television ads, watching the papers for special deals and offerings, we can keep up in an ever changing market place. Lee Iacocca former chairman and CEO of the Chrysler Corporation once said,
"In business, you either lead: follow, or get out of the way." When it comes to customer service be a leader, set the standard and make the other guy follow you. If you are not the lead dog, then the view never changes.

A few years ago I made reservations at a nice restaurant for my wife and I to celebrate our twentieth wedding anniversary. I took the time to arrange everything; the table, meal, flowers, champagne, and a special cake for dessert. The day before our special night out, I called the restaurant to request a balloon bouquet to accompany the flowers. After I finished speaking the manager seemed a bit puzzled and informed me that they had no such reservation made in my name. The manager also informed me that they were completely booked the rest of the week; and the earliest he could fit me in was later the following week. I even explained to him whom I had talked with and when I had called, but it made no difference they were not going to honor my request.

After I hung up the phone I frantically flipped through the phone book for somewhere else to go. I finally located an establishment not as fancy as the first, but still located on the waterfront and explained my frustration and dilemma to the girl on the other end of the line. She asked me to hold for a moment, then: the manager came on the line and asked me what they could do to help. I once again explained what had happened to the manager and simply asked if they could fit us in for a dinner reservation the following night (our anniversary)
"Will 7:00pm be all right" the manger asked
"It sure will be," I said "That is the same time we had dinner on our wedding night"
"Thank you Mr. Briggs we look forward to seeing you both tomorrow night."

I had all but given up on the special events I had planned with the first restaurant since there would not be enough time for them to arrange it all, so my wife and I went out the next night just expecting to have dinner, Boy were we surprised! Upon arriving at the restaurant we were identified by the hostess who took us immediately to our table by the window with an un-obstructed view of Puget Sound. Waiting for us at the table was a beautiful bouquet of flowers and balloons, a bottle of champagne on ice, and a small table top banner that read Happy 20th Anniversary.

The whole evening went off without a hitch; except for my wife's love of champagne and the effects of tiny bubbles. For

one evening we were royalty, spoiled by what seemed to be our
own personal wait staff, but there is more.
Just when we thought it was over there was yet another
surprise, a beautiful cake for dessert and endless wishes of
Happy Anniversary. It is a memory we will never forget.

By being a better choice to our customers, we too can be
someone they will never forget. I can not remember where I
heard it from but I once heard that if a customer is happy with
the service they received they will tell at least five others; but,
if they are dissatisfied they will tell at least twelve other people.
That is more than a two to one ratio of negativity. Can you
afford that kind of customer service and survive in business?
NO! Whether it is one customer or twelve, any amount of
negativity can be devastating.

I want you to take a few minutes and list at least three other companies that offer the same product or service you do. If you truly know your local marketplace this should be a very easy task, if not, then you have already given your potential customers a reason to choose someone else.

Once you have finished your list, write down five attributes that make you the better choice; someone they will never forget. If you can not list at least five reasons illustrating what makes you a better choice, then you need to re-think your approach to customer service. Remember, in today's marketplace the customer is bombarded with choices. Therefore we need to step up our efforts with customer service, be the leader so that you too will be someone your customers will never forget.

Keep in mind that location, product availability, accessibility and affordability are important.

If you lack the most basic customer service skills you may as well close your doors now.

When we lack basic customer service we greatly diminish our chances for business survival. Remember the busy business district? Can you survive in a marketplace where the customer has so many choices facing them?

Because the customer has a **CHOICE,**
We must be the **BETTER** choice.

Chapter III.

<u>Because the Customer has Sensibilities.</u>

"What is the best way to approach the customer?"
Eric

Back over at Sternhaven Incorporated International Eric once
again sat down for his weekly meeting with
Mr. Sternhaven.

"Mr. Sternhaven Sir" Eric asked. "What is the best way to
approach the customer?"
Puffing on his usual cigar Mr. Sternhaven paused for a
moment, let go a large plum of smoke, smiled and said.
"IDIOTS"

"Idiots?" Eric asked.

"That's right" Mr. Sternhaven said. "Let me tell you my boy, customers are idiots. Most of them wouldn't understand what happened to them until it was too late."

"Wouldn't that offend them?" Eric asked.

"Not if you talk real fast my boy and use a lot of big words to confuse them." Mr. Sternhaven said. "Do not ask the customer too many questions." He continued. "And do not forget my motto my boy. **SELL!, SELL!, SELL!,** get that contract signed at any cost, the bigger the better I always say. Who cares what the customer wants." Mr. Sternhaven announced boldly.

"I understand sir." Eric replied

*   *   *

It was another Monday morning at Smith's Apparel Wholesalers: Jamie came into the office with a certain bounce to her step, and a smile that would brighten the darkest of days.

"Goooooood Morning! Mr. Smith." Jamie said.

"Well good morning to you too Jamie." Mr. Smith replied. "You seem to be an extra good mood today Jamie. What's up?"

"I just can not wait to hear what you have to say about the customer today." Jamie said. "I know it's not Christmas Mr. Smith," Jamie continued. "But after our last meeting I just had to watch the Miracle on 34th Street again. I now fully understand what you meant about the customers needs and choices."

"That's Great Jamie!" Mr. Smith replied. "But Jamie let me ask you this. When you go shopping do you make a list?"

"Of course I do." Jamie said. "You know I have to be sensible about what I buy."

"Why's that?" Mr. Smith asked.

"Because I have other obligations that I also need to take care of." Jamie replied.

"That's right Jamie." Mr. Smith said. "Remember Jamie" he continued. "That the customer has a need and a choice."

"Yes Mr. Smith."

"Well Jamie, because of that they too are sensible shoppers. Jamie," Mr. Smith asked. "Have you ever read the book <u>Raving Fans</u> by Ken Blanchard & Sheldon Bowles?"

"No." said Jamie.

"Well in the book <u>Raving Fans</u>." Mr. Smith continued. "It says that we need to fully understand our customers needs, and put their needs first. Which brings me to my third rule of customer service, and remember."
"Because the customer has **SENSIBILITIES,** we must be **CONSIDERATE.**"

"That is why Jamie, we take the time to fully understand our customers needs, and put their needs first."

*   *   *

When a customer walks through your door, what is your first thought about who you see? More importantly, what is their first impression of you?

Are you BOLD, PUSHY, LOUD, GRABBY and ARROGANT?
Or are you
WARM, HELPFUL, KNOWLEDGEBLE, CONSIDERATE and HUMBLE?

"Because the customer has **SENSIBILITIES,** we must be **CONSIDERATE.**"

If you can learn to use all of the above attributes, except grabby and pushy to your advantage then you're on the right track. Most customers are willing to open up and share information about themselves if and when they feel the customer service individual understands what they need, and respects who they are. This helps create a strong customer and customer service report. This is why more and more companies take the time to ask you personal questions, but there is more than just asking questions and filling out forms to fully understand who your customers are. Take a few minutes and get to know them on a more personal level. You do not need to know their whole life story, just a few tidbits that will help you understand more about them, and their needs.

One of my biggest pet peeves in shopping is when I go into a place and the sales person treats me like I am an IDIOT. I no longer stick around for their "help" and abuse, I just simply walk out and never go back.

A good customer service professional has full knowledge of the product or service they offer, and is capable of answering any questions you may ask.

DO THEY REALLY?

Remember, it's what we learn after we know it all that really counts.

As I stated earlier, customers are becoming more and more savvy about the products they seek. With all of the new technology that is available to them today, consumers often research any item they want from audio visual to automobiles. Often in most cases they know more about the product they seek than the so-called professional they are talking with. This is why we must know our products and services in and out, backwards and forwards, like Katy did at the electronics store where I bought my camera. The old saying "If you can't dazzle them with brilliance, then baffle them with B.S." no longer holds true. Katy knew her stuff because she was going to school, learning photography and was able to share her knowledge in a professional and helpful manner.

Have you ever walked into a variety store that sells everything from automobile products to clothes to groceries? You know, that one stop shop that sells a lot of everything and a whole lot of nothing. Did you ever take the time to ask an employee for information about a certain product and watched them give you the "deer in the headlights look". When they finally come out of shock from being confronted with a question, you can expect one of the following reactions!

A. They have the answer and know the product.

B. Take the time to read you the product tag, remember we're idiots and cannot read.

C. They say "I don't know and then run for help."

Most of the time you can count on B or C, this is because most super stores do not need knowledgeable sales staff. They just need a body to fill a position. **Please,** Do not assume for one minute that I think every employee at a super store is not experienced and knowledgeable, but sadly all too many times the ratio usually stands at 3:10.

When you are lucky enough to get the one employee who knows their merchandise and all of the benefits it offers it is like a breath of fresh air. It is for this reason that we must know our own products and services, so that we do not come across to our own customers like the deer in the headlights and become customer service road kill.

For the most part, Super stores usually have three main attributes: A great location, large selection of products that are reasonably priced and they are all located in a convenient one stop shop. Walk into one of these stores and you will find yourself becoming a ghost shopper, roaming isle to isle never seen or even acknowledge. Why? They are to busy either talking to other staff members, or avoiding the inevitable customer service confrontation; the question. Can I help you? It is because of this that they typically lack in customer service. For them, volume is the key to success. Thus continuous training is set aside because it takes money to keep their staff sharp in the art of quality customer service.

For large numbers of us who work either for a smaller business or a sole proprietor, we must remember that everyone who walks through our door is important, because of their unique individual impact. So let me ask you once again. When a customer walks through your door, what is you first thought of them? Most importantly to ask yourself, what is their first impression of you?

The customer is there because they have a **NEED, A CHOICE and SENSIBILITIES** and because of this we must be **CONSIDERATE.**

Think back to the old saying "Treat others the way that you would like to be treated." Understand in today's tough marketplace the customer has probably already done their homework before they even get to you. So take the time to understand your customers needs, and realize that you are not the only game in town. Treat your customers with respect and do not patronize them. Be helpful and considerate and you will be successful.

"Because the customer has **SENSIBILITIES,** we must be **CONSIDERATE.**"

Chapter IV.

Because the Customer has Urgency.

"Congratulations Jamie, you just got a raise"
Mr. Smith

It was another Monday morning at Sternhaven Incorporated International (Stinc Int'l) as Eric sat patiently waiting for Mr. Sternhaven to arrive for their weekly meeting. Recently, Mr. Sternhaven had fired a Sales Executive who had been with the company for twelve years because of his slumping sales. He was also getting uneasy with Eric's slow start as a Sales Executive. Eric had been doing everything Mr. Sternhaven told him so far, but the customers were just not responding. Especially a longtime client, The Borden Company. Finally Mr. Sternhaven arrived at his office, in a cloud of cigar smoke; as he passed Eric he said nothing: but motioned for Eric to follow.

Once in Mr. Sternhavens office Eric sat and watched as Mr. Sternhaven puffed on his cigar and read a file that had been left on his desk. Mr. Sternhaven took one last puff from his cigar as he stared across the desk at his young protégé, sitting nervously. Moments finally passed when Mr. Sternhaven spoke to Eric. "Eric my boy, I see here in your last sales report that you failed to close two deals, Why?"

"Mr. Sternhaven Sir." Eric said. "The customers told me they had time constraints, and if we could not meet their urgent request they would go somewhere else."

Mr. Sternhaven responded sharply, "I DO NOT CARE HOW SOON THEY NEED IT!" he continued by saying firmly. "Promise them they'll get it when they want it. Get the contract signed. Do whatever it takes to get the deal done, DO YOU UNDERSTAND ME?!"

"Mr. Sternhaven" Eric asked. "What happens when they call and ask about it? What do I tell them?"

"Eric" Mr. Sternhaven responded. "Tell them that you will get back to them soon, then move on to something else. Do not waste anymore of your time." He continued by saying. "There is always tomorrow to do the final details and follow up."

It was a warm sunny Monday morning when Jamie arrived at Smith's Apparel Wholesalers. Jamie looked around the parking lot and then glanced at her watch. "Was I late for work?" She wondered. "The parking lot is never this full so early in the morning" As soon as Jamie walked into the office everyone cheered, and Jamie noticed a banner hanging from the ceiling that read.

Congratulations Jamie

Jamie stood there in disbelief for a moment not knowing what to say while everyone continued to cheer.

Suddenly Mr. Smith appeared out of nowhere, smiling like a man who just won the lottery.

"JAMIE!" he shouted, "We found out Friday at noon that we got the Borden account, they are coming over this morning to sign the contract. What made them change their mind? How did you do it?" Mr. Smith said.

"Mr. Smith" Jamie said, "Lets go for coffee in the break room where it is quiet and I will tell you all about it." Once they arrived in the break room and had their cup of coffee in hand, Jamie explained to Mr. Smith what happened.

"Well Mr. Smith it's like this," Jamie said, "I remembered about our earlier discussion: About the customers needs, choices and sensibilities. Last Thursday I had a meeting with Mr. Borden. He is a very difficult man to get a hold of. Once we were able to sit down together and talk, he said that he was having problems with his current supplier and that they needed a certain product by this Wednesday.

I told him that I would look into it for him, and asked him if I was able to make it happen, would they sign a long term agreement with us?" Jamie continued. "So I went to lunch letting Mr. Borden know that I would get back to him Friday

Morning. As I sat down for lunch, I overheard a conversation at the next table."

"Go on" Mr. Smith said.

Jamie continued explaining, "There were two men sitting at the next table who had been over shipped the very product that Mr. Borden's Company desperately needed, so I asked them about it. They told me that their supplier, Sternhaven Incorporated would not allow a return authorization, and that they were in dire straits with their boss.
So Mr. Smith, I made them an offer they could not refuse. I called Mr. Borden back to let him know that not only could I get him his product, but also that it would be delivered before noon on Friday. I then called a friend of mine at Briggs Trucking Company and requested an expedited shipment to the Borden Company first thing Friday morning. That Mr. Smith" Jamie concluded. "Is how we arrived at this point in time"

Mr. Smith sat speechless for a moment or so, just looking at Jamie not knowing quite what to say. Suddenly he blurted out so even the people in the office could hear.

"Jamie, that is outstanding work!"

"I was planning today to share with you rule number four but now I guess that it is no longer necessary."

"OH PLEASE! Mr. Smith do tell me," Jamie said. "PLEASE"

"OK Jamie, Ok" Mr. Smith continued.
"I guess it would be un-fair not to share my fourth rule of
customer service with you Jamie, so remember:"
"Because the customer has **URGENCY,**
we must be **QUICK.**"

"Jamie, sometimes our customers are in a hurry, just like
Mr. Borden, and we need to step up our efforts, just like you
did for Mr. Borden and his company. Keeping on top of a
situation and communicating with our customers really makes
a difference. Thanks to your quick-thinking and your customer
care urgency, The Borden Company is dropping Sternhaven
Incorporated International and going with our company."

"Congratulations Jamie, you just got a raise."

FAST food, *FAST* pass, *FAST* lane, *FAST* cash. Yes, we live in a society where we want things *FAST*. Our customers also have expectations of speedy service, but then do we give up the quality of customer service they deserve or desire, probably. Now you may never be in the right place at the right time as Jamie was in the story; but knowing your customers need for urgency and doing the appropriate follow-up will insure that the job gets done, and the customer will be back.

Urgency happens in many aspects of business, from a regular client who calls you desperate for product they shorted themselves when they placed their last order, or the customer who walks through your door looking for that last minute item for a dinner party they are hosting. Urgency, what about the retail store getting ready to release the latest high-tech devise to hit the market; or the executive that needs to get an oil change while they take their lunch break. Everywhere we turn, businesses are gearing up for people on the go, but are falling short when it comes to the personal touch called: customer service.

Too many businesses claim they have speedy service simply to lure customers, but then fall flat when it comes to fulfilling that statement, that also falls under the category of false advertising, but that's another story for a different book.

There is a retail tire chain in the western United States called Les Schwab Tire, their motto clearly states.
"When you pull in, we'll come running"
Les Schwab Tire held themselves to a high standard of speedy service and fulfilled that promise day in, day out. I remember

once pulling into a Les Schwab with a flat tire, by the time I parked the car and opened my door a tire technician stood waiting to greet me. Alan introduced himself, politely asked me what level of service I would be requiring that day. I stated that my rear tire had started to go flat and that I needed it to be repaired. Alan invited me to go inside and check in with the counter while he fixed the tire. As I walked inside the building there were three other customers being helped by the staff at the counter, One of the staff members instantly acknowledged my presence and said, "someone will be right with you, please feel free to help yourself to some fresh coffee."

I had no sooner poured a cup of coffee when a staff member approached me and asked if he could be of assistance. As we walked to the counter I explained what happened and that Alan was already taking care of it. Before we even reached the counter, Alan appeared from the shop, smiling and said. "Sir your tire is fixed, it was just a faulty valve stem which I replaced." he thanked me for coming in and then returned to continue his previous duties.

Les Schwab did not charge me for that simple repair, but instead thanked me for my patronage and asked me to keep them in mind for my future tire needs. I am very proud to say that I have been a loyal Les Schwab Tire customer now for over twenty years.

That's what I call service, customer service. A positive experience: where I felt welcome and important to them, willing to do repeat business with them, for life.

What happens though when our experience is not so positive? Read on and you'll find out.

Special door buster sales and the Holiday's can throw the best retailers into a tail spin, people are in a hurry and have no patience for the lackadaisical sales staff that await to greet them, and then their total lack of quality customer service. How many times have you gone into a retail outlet and had to wait for the employee to finish a call before they will help you? In all honesty, I have lost count. I do remember a few years ago when my wife and I were doing some holiday shopping, we had gathered a large amount of items and then joined the line to check out.

Once we finally arrived at the register we were greeted by the clerk who just finished up a call, as we set our items down the clerk started to arrange them in such a way to make it easier to ring them up.

Suddenly the phone rang, she answered the call and asked the person on the other end of the line if she could be of assistance to her. As my wife and I stood there in disbelief that the caller was more important to the clerk than us, she set the phone down and ran off to seek out the information the caller requested. A few minutes passed when the clerk re-appeared picked up the phone, gave the caller the information they sought, thanked them for calling and hung up the phone. No sooner had she started to help us the second time, when the phone rang once again.
That's right! You guessed it, she answered it.

As the clerk once again rushed to answer the phone, she told the caller that she would have to check the floor and see if the product was still available, as she set the phone down and started to walk away once again, I spoke up.

"Miss, my wife and I along with all these other customers have been waiting awhile to be helped, and I'm sure like us they have other places to go"

The clerk swung around and informed me that the caller was an important customer and continued to walk off.

I turned to the line of customers that had formed behind my wife and I then stated very firmly.

"Apparently those of us standing in line with our money in-hand are not important enough to this store"

With that my wife and I, along with half the people behind us in line dropped our items and left. My wife and I walked away leaving behind a sale of more than $300.00; but not before I reached over the counter and hung up the phone to the cheers of the customers behind me.

When it comes to customer service, do not be distracted by trivial things, you may find yourself at the end of a wrong number, or staring into the eyes of an angry customer.

Urgency happens in so many ways with customers. How we choose to handle it sets us apart from the rest.

Picture a Nascar race; the drivers are the customers and the pit crews are the customer service professionals. We must all work together in a urgent manner to get the customer going as quickly as possible. In a race it's the difference between winning and losing, in customer service it is the difference between gaining a loyal customer or losing them to our competition.

In the story Jamie just happened to be in the right place at the right time. She seized the moment turning an unstable customer situation into a solid foundation that would allow her to build on in the future. Giving her the sale, and her company a solid relationship with that customer.

As for my wife and I, we ended up spending $500 with another store in the same mall. Then we returned to the first store and explained our discontent with the clerks handling of the situation to the store manager and how they lost our business all from a lack of customer service.

Chapter V.

Because the customer is Unique.

"Your promotion depends on it"
Mr. Sternhaven

Tensions were running high Monday morning at Sternhaven Incorporated International. Mr. Sternhaven was growing increasingly irritated with his sales staff including his newest protégé` Eric. In the last week alone five customers had jumped ship leaving Mr. Sternhaven scratching his head and asking, Why? Without enough customers he had to fire three more long term Sales Executives along with a dozen support staff.

"Mr. Sternhaven" Eric asked nervously. "I know that I am new to this game and lack the experience the others have. Why did you keep me and let them go?"

"It's simple Eric my boy, There is still hope that I can mold you into the kind of salesperson I expect." Mr. Sternhaven said. "Eric my boy when I look at you I see a cold-blooded calculated man who thinks of himself first."
Eric sat up and smiled. Mr. Sternhaven continued.
"And I like that in a man. It is what has gotten me this far. Remember Eric to **SELL, SELL, SELL,** get that contract signed no matter what the cost, the bigger, the better I always say, and Eric my boy as far as the customers go, they are all the same. They want my products, and they have money to spend. Tons of money. Some of course more than others, but its money just the same. So remember to **SELL, SELL, SELL.**"

"I understand Mr. Sternhaven" Eric said with confidence.

"Now Eric, I am expecting great things from you, and I know you won't let me down. Now go get'em my boy, your promotion depends on it."

"YES SIR! Mr. Sternhaven sir"

"Oh, and one more question Eric. Do you know a girl named Jamie Easystreet?" Mr. Sternhaven asked.

"Well yes Sir Mr. Sternhaven, Jamie and I graduated college together. Why do you ask?"

*   *   *

As Jamie arrived for work and her weekly Monday morning meeting with Mr. Smith, she noticed an empty parking lot and a moving truck in front of the building.

Jamie rushed inside to see what was happening.
"Mr. Smith, What's going on? What's happening?"
Jamie asked frantically.

"Good morning to you to Jamie" Mr. Smith laughed.
"I have some great news. We signed two more new clients last
week with long term contracts, all because of you Jamie."

"That's nice Mr. Smith" Jamie said, "but it still does not
explain why the movers are here."

"Hang on Jamie, hang on." Mr. Smith explained.
"With the new customers we have, this old office is just to
small and out-dated Jamie." Mr. Smith continued.
"We are moving into a new office and the movers are here just
to gather up our files and a few special pieces of old furniture."

"But what about our weekly meetings in the break room and
my old desk?" Jamie asked

"Not to worry Jamie," Mr. Smith said. "Everything is taken
care of. Here let us go to the break room one more time before
we leave this old office for our weekly talk." Mr. Smith said.

As they arrived in the break room they grabbed their usual cup
of coffee and took a seat at the old table. Everything seemed to
be in its place, Jamie smiled.

"So what is on your mind Jamie?" Mr. Smith asked.

"Well Mr. Smith" Jamie said "In past meetings you taught me that the customers have a need and a choice. And you also reminded me that they have sensibilities and urgency. Does that mean that we treat every customer the same?"

"Of course not Jamie," Mr. Smith chuckled. "When you were in college Jamie did everyone take the same courses?"

"NO." said Jamie.

"Why's that?" Mr. Smith inquired.

"We all had different class requirements and different needs based on what we wanted to be after we graduated." Jamie said.
Mr. Smith smiled, took a sip of his coffee and then said, "Because we are all different Jamie, we need to treat each customer different, here is rule number five."
"Because the customer is **UNIQUE,** we must be **FLEXIBLE.**"
"Jamie each customer is unique, each with their own special needs. That is why we need to change our approach accordingly so we can make every transaction a positive one. Jamie would you give a drowning man a glass of water? Or would you give him your hand to help him out of the water?" Mr. Smith asked.

*   *   *

They say that America is the melting pot of the world, each culture, religion and home is unique to those who live there.

The customers that you encounter on a daily basis are just as unique with their own special kind of needs. This is why we must move with the emotional tide and change our course for a successful customer journey.

Remember back from chapter one: "Because the customer has a need" This is true more than ever, because each and every customer is unique we must be flexible. Here, let us look at it this way: you are at a state fair. There are rides, animals, crafts, games and food. The only problem is if you have seen one state fair you pretty much have seen them all with very little difference between them. How many times have you seen a food establishment that has a large variety of items on the menu, the answer is: you don't. There are typically different stands each serving one to four items, though specializing in one. This is ok for them because at most fairs, food is not the main reason why people go. Food is a temporary fix that will help keep people there for longer stays.

In this case most people at a state fair will settle on the quickest thing they can find to eat: hamburgers, hotdogs, corndogs, ice cream, you get the picture. **But!** What if you have customers who have food restrictions such as allergies, culture, religious or even vegetarian needs, how many of those potential customers would you lose?

"Because the customer is unique, we must be flexible." Now on the flip side to state fairs are amusement parks such as Disneyland, Six Flags, Cedar Point, Sea World and many others whose customer base reaches into the millions annually. They are visited by people from all around the world so they

have had to change with the times, realizing the uniqueness of each and every customer who enters their gates.
"Because the customer is unique, we must be flexible."

Large superstore chains make it easy to appeal to the mass public, open longer hours, or even all night, they typically rely on the volume of customers for their business letting customer service slowly slip away. This reminds me of the old saying:
"The bigger they are, the harder they fall."
What if you are a specialty shop? Whether it be retail or manufacturing, you then narrow your customer base by at least 50%, and because you are not the only shop out there your customer now has other choices to consider also.
"Because the customer is unique, we must be flexible."
And because every customer is unique you need to work that much harder in order to keep your customers coming back.

Can a company survive when it has a limited menu, product or manufacturing line, or is limited by what service it performs?

Yes it can. They just need to work longer and harder just to survive the day to day issues that face them. Typically these type shops specialize for a select few customers mostly in manufacturing, and because they have worked with them before; or they have an ongoing working contract.
However, have you ever seen a fast food joint with a limited menu survive and in fact do very well? I have. There is a chain of hamburger joints in California called, "In-N-Out" burgers that has less than ten items on their menu and they put out one of the best burgers you will ever have. What's their secret to success? Simplicity, by keeping their menu simple they are able

to appeal to a much larger customer base, each with their own unique concept of what they want and how they want it. Not to mention the fact that everything is home made, and they have fast friendly service along with a clean neat environment. "Because the customer is unique, we must be flexible."

Take a look sometime at a fast food, or sit down restaurant's menu the next time you eat out. There is a good chance that somewhere on the menu it will read "No substitutions." But what if I do not want it that way, then either I order something else or find a different place to eat. That is what usually happens.

"Hold the pickles, hold the lettuce, special orders don't upset us, all we ask is that you let us serve it your way."

One of the most memorable lines in advertising, and Burger King hit a home run with customer service because of it. "All we ask is that you let us serve it **Your Way**" WOW! my way, because I'm unique and they're flexible. Burger King recognized early on that their customers were unique and not everyone wanted their food fixed the same way, so flexibility became the norm. Now you do not need to be a food establishment just to be flexible. These were just a couple of examples to show you just how easy it can be when you recognize that everyone has a slightly different take on what they want, and how they want it.

In today's tough marketplace everyone is jockeying for position with the customer base by trying to out do the other guy. Bigger and better does not always work, re-think your position, slow down, simplify and realize that every customer is unique.

No matter what you are selling, supplying, manufacturing or servicing, Think of your customers needs first and how you can best serve those needs for them now and also in the future.

"Because the customer is **UNIQUE,**
we must be **FLEXIBLE.**"

Chapter VI.

<u>Because the Customer has High Expectations.</u>

"for us to go the extra mile…"
Mr. Smith

Sternhaven Incorporated International was in turmoil. More and more customers were getting tired by the lack of customer service they were receiving. As of Monday morning eight more customers had dropped Stinc Int'l as their primary supplier. Mr. Sternhaven's young protégé` Eric was at his wits end. Eric kept hearing the name Jamie Easystreet in conversations with clients, and now knew why Mr. Sternhaven had asked about her. Jamie was cutting into Eric's business and gaining customer momentum in the market place, leaving Eric to explain why to Mr. Sternhaven.

As Eric sat outside of Mr. Sternhaven's office awaiting his weekly meeting with Mr. Sternhaven, he could hear through the door the level of anger that Mr. Sternhaven was expressing by the volume of his voice and the choice of his words. Eric had never heard him so angry.

Eric knew once he stepped inside Mr. Sternhaven's office he would have to think fast on who to blame for his recent lack of success, after all he knew it could not be his fault. The call finally came and Eric stepped into Mr. Sternhaven's office.

"SIT DOWN!" Mr. Sternhaven demanded.

"I demand an explanation, faltering sales, customers leaving and if I hear the name Jamie Easystreet one more time, HEADS WILL ROLL!" Mr. Sternhaven yelled sharply pounding his fist on the desk.

"Mr. Sternhaven, Sir" Eric said
"I have done everything that you have told me so far, but it is like I need to baby sit the clients. What do they expect from me?" Eric asked.

"Your job! Eric, they expect you to do your job, just like I do" Mr. Sternhaven screamed.

"YYYYes Sir" Eric said timidly. "But the customers are so demanding" he continued "What should I do?" asked Eric.

"Eric, the solution is simple" Mr. Sternhaven snapped.
"Step it up, or pack it up."

Excitement was in the air at Smith's Apparel Wholesalers as Mr. Smith waited patiently for Jamie to arrive for their weekly 7:00 am talk. It was 9:00 am. Mr. Smith was growing concerned, it was unlike Jamie to be late. Jamie rushed into the room catching her breath, she proceeded to explain.

"Mr. Smith I am sorry for being late, I know you expected me first thing this morning, but I had an urgent matter to clear up with a new customer. Remember Mr. Smith"
Jamie continued. "Because the customer has a need, we have a job to do. Well Mr. Smith, this customers needs could not wait."

"I understand" Mr. Smith said. "Did everything work out ok?"

"Yes Mr. Smith" Jamie replied.

"Jamie" Mr. Smith asked. "What exactly was the urgent matter that could not wait until later?"

"Well Mr. Smith" Jamie said. "I promised a customer that I would get the newest catalog to them Friday so they could have them in time to look over before a purchasing meeting they were having at 8:00 am this morning. I found out late Friday afternoon from the printer that the catalogs would be delayed due to a problem with their machinery, and that they would not be ready until 6:00 am Monday morning."
Catching her breath, Jamie continued to explain.
"So this morning I drove over to the printers first thing, picked up the catalogs and then rushed them to the customer in time for their meeting."

"Jamie, why didn't you call me?" Mr. Smith asked.

Blushing Jamie replied.
"I forgot my cell phone at home." They both chuckled.

"Jamie" Mr. Smith said. "Once again you went beyond typical customer service and really stepped up to the plate. We know the customers all have different needs, choices, sensibilities and urgency, and yes every customer is unique. But there is one thing they all have in common. Every customer whether they spend a little or a lot all have high expectations of the sales person they are in contact with. So Jamie, remember rule number six."
"Because the customer has high **EXPECTATIONS,** we must **EXCEL.**"

Mr. Smith continued.
"Jamie, today you proved how important it is for us to excel, how important it is for us to go the extra mile. Your customer had high expectations of receiving the catalogs in time for their meeting, and in a time of crisis when a problem occurred you did not stop there. Jamie you went the extra mile, accelerating yourself to customer care excellence."

"Thank you Mr. Smith" Jamie said.

"OH! I almost forgot" Mr. Smith added.
"Speaking of accelerating, I wanted to give you keys to your new company car."

*   *   *

Communication, caring, follow up, honesty, these are just a few things that customers want to see when they deal with a customer service professional, but is there more…

What does the customer expect from us? Is it low expectations? No.
What does the customer expect form us? Is it medium expectations? **NO!**
Then what does the customer expect from us? Is it high expectations? **YES!!**
"Because the customer has high expectations, we must excel."

Steven K. Scott author of the book "Mentored by a Millionaire" refers to the vision and plan for success as a Porsche, not just any Porsche, but a super charged high performance machine capable of accelerating us to our goal. Just because the customer is only a mile off. Do we stop there? NO!
That is when we must go the extra mile, taking our foot off the cruise control of customer service mediocrity and accelerate ourselves to our goal. In this case our goal is ultimate customer service.

Remember back in chapter three when I asked you, "When a customer walks through your door, what is your first thought of them? Most importantly: What is their first impression of you?"
You never have a second chance to make a first impression.

Let your customers know from the start that they can count on you through every step of the way to make their experience a truly unforgettable one; That they can count on you again in the future. Going the extra mile for your customer really pays off, it shows to them that you care about their business now and in the future. Because of that simple gesture you will be rewarded with what every successful customer service professional wants: Referrals, referrals and more referrals. If you do not think that referrals are important you may as well close your doors now and save yourself a lot of grief and money.

How many times have you bought something only to have it break, shrink, stop working or what ever else could go wrong with it? You take the time to return it to the store, get a replacement or a refund and go on your way. It is a simple process that happens hundreds of times throughout the day. What happens though when you need to go right to the source, the manufacturer? How do they deal with it? How do they go the extra mile? By listening to the customer and understanding their needs, by being flexible, considerate, and by living up the customers high expectations.

In 1986 when my daughter was born, my wife and I struggled just to make ends meet. Using clothe diapers would have cost to much with the extra laundry expense or even the use of a diaper service was beyond our means. So we settled on the use of disposable diapers instead. One day my wife reached for a diaper and the tape strips had no adhesive on them, she wanted to throw it away but I suggested that we mail it back to the manufacturer Kimberly Clark with a letter explaining the problem. Ten days had passed when we received a response thanking us for bringing this problem to their attention and that they were passing it on to the appropriate department for review. Two weeks later we received another letter form Kimberly Clark, much thicker than the first thanking us once again for our time in bringing this problem to their attention.

Upon investigation the manufacturer had found a flaw in the processing where some of the adhesive strips were not getting any adhesive coating. They were able to correct the problem saving them a lot of money and embarrassment. Kimberly Clark thanked us by sending coupons for some free merchandise and many more coupons for discounts on future purchases.

We took just a few minutes of our time to let Kimberly Clark know about a problem. They went the extra mile by insuring complete customer satisfaction, and responded with generosity, presenting us with a plethora of coupons and the thanks of a grateful company.

So you see it is a simple process to go the extra mile, and it does not take a major corporation to do it, it is within all of us. Every sales person, store clerk, mobile service tech, customer service individual, or even the person behind the scenes can make an impact as long as they care about the customers needs. When you look back at all the stories I have told you throughout the book, you can see what the difference is when you go the extra mile for your customers or fall short of reaching the finish line. There is one common thread that holds all of the successful companies together, and that is their employee's went the extra mile to ensure complete customer service satisfaction.

How many times have you stopped working with a customer
once a sale is done or a service preformed?
Or has a sales person stop working with you once your
purchase was complete? Did you feel abandoned?
If we do not take care of our customers, someone else will.
Treat others the way that you would want to be treated.

Don't just cruise through customer service, ACCELORATE
yourself, put yourself out front, set the standards and make
others live up to your expectations. Be like Jamie in the story,
follow through with your suppliers to ensure your customers
get the service they deserve. Once the sale is completed follow
up with your customers to make sure that they are satisfied.
It is not hard to go the extra mile when you set your sights
further down the road.
"Because the customer has high Expectations,
we must excel."

Chapter VII.

Because the customer has Influence.

"Congratulations Jamie…"
Mr. Smith

It was black Monday at Sternhaven Incorporated International. Mr. Sternhaven had been going around handing out pink slips all morning. Business had hit an all time low, creditors were bearing down, the bank refused to loan anymore money, and Mr. Sternhaven had already closed four out of his five offices in four other countries, leaving just his head office in operation.

Meanwhile Eric was in his office with a new client scrambling to get this deal signed. It was a huge deal that would generate top dollars and bring some much needed relief to the company. Down the hall Mr. Sternhaven sat in his office tired and

distraught over the recent events. He looked endlessly at a picture of himself and his office staff standing in front of his first office. Mr. Sternhaven was reflecting how simple things were, and how good business had been in that small overcrowded office so many years ago. Suddenly there came a pounding knock at the door, Mr. Sternhaven jumped to his feet and said.
"Come in Eric and give me the good news."
It wasn't Eric at the door but the potential client, and he was VERY angry.

"I have never been treated like this before." The client screamed. "I came to Sternhaven Incorporated International because I had an urgent need, and your so called "salesman" treated me like I was an idiot. I tried to tell him what I needed, but he just kept talking fast and using a lot of big words. I tried countless times to explain to him my unique situation, and he just kept trying to get me to sign some sort of contract that I did not understand. I then tried to explain to him the urgency of my need, but he still would not listen. I told him that I expected more from your company and he just said, sign here and you will get more."

Stunned at the man's anger, Mr. Sternhaven said softly. "I am sorry, will you please sit down so we can discuss your needs? I am sure we can work something out."

"Certainly NOT!" the client replied."I expected more from your company, and like they say. Attitude reflects leadership." The client continued by saying. "Stinc Int'l will not get my business today or anytime in the future. In fact when I go to next month's Trade Convention I am going to spread the word about how I was treated here."

With that the client turned and left Mr. Sternhaven's office passing Eric in the hallway as Eric made his way to see Mr. Sternhaven. Mr. Sternhaven's office door was still open when Eric arrived.

"Come in Eric and have a seat." Mr. Sternhaven said calmly, "close the door behind you please."

As Eric sat down he proceeded to explain what had just happened. "Mr. Sternhaven Sir," Eric said. "I did everything possible to..."

"STOP Right there Eric! Mr. Sternhaven interrupted, I have heard enough and I am tired of all the excuses. Eric when I hired you right out of college my expectations of you and your ability were high. Maybe I expected too much of you. You were short tempered, arrogant, competitive and very out spoken, qualities I like to see in a sales executive. Eric, I tried everything possible to mold you into a top contender, but you failed me miserably. Due to your arrogance and because of your incompetence, sales are down, way down. Customers have left and with what that last potential client told me, the customers have a lot of influence. Eric my boy I have no choice but to cut my losses before it is ultimately too late. Give me the keys to your company car, I expect you to clean out your office and be gone before the end of the day."

*   *   *

At Smith's Apparel Wholesalers Jamie waited in the break room for her weekly talk with Mr. Smith when he suddenly appeared.
"JAMIE!" Mr. Smith said exuberantly.
"I just thought you might want to see this."

"See what?" Jamie asked.

"Jamie, remember a few weeks ago when the reporter was here asking questions and taking pictures?"

"Yes Mr. Smith, who could forget that day," Jamie said. "I looked awful and he kept taking my picture, why do you ask?"

"Because of this Jamie," Mr. Smith said (holding a trade magazine with Jamie's picture on the front) "and look what it says."
Jamie sat there for a moment stunned as she read the front cover headline.
"Meet Jamie Easystreet of Smith's Apparel Wholesalers, Wholesalers Trade Sales Executive of the year 2003."

"I do not know what to say," Jamie said. "I'm speechless"

"That's ok Jamie," Mr. Smith replied.
"I'll talk, you just sit there and enjoy your cup of coffee. In 2000 when I hired you right out of college, my company had grown enough that I needed help in sales. I received dozens of resumes that spring, some of the applicants came highly recommended with greater experience which was a plus. They also had some bad habits in business which I could not tolerate. Then I came across your resume and cover letter:

it was simple and talked about your hard work, how you volunteer in the community: It also talked about your sense of teamwork and how we need to work together. After I read it I knew in my heart that you were the right person to represent my company; you hold yourself to the same high ideals I do, and that you realize it takes teamwork, people coming together for the success of all. I know now that hiring you was the best decision I ever made: who you are Jamie, really makes a difference. I expected good things from, and you have not only met those expectations many times over, you exceeded them."

"I am glad that I have been a positive influence Mr. Smith," Jamie said. "It is really a simple concept Mr. Smith" she continued, "When we learn and fully understand that the customers have needs, choices, sensibilities and urgency, And that every customer is unique with high expectations, then we will always be successful."

"Your right Jamie," Mr. Smith said. "But there is one more rule that is most important of all, my seventh rule. Because the customer has **INFLUENCE,** we have the hope of **MORE** customers."

"Jamie" Mr. Smith continued. "Due to your customer care excellence along with the customers influence, our customer base could not be stronger. We have grown so much, and it is all because of your hard work. Also with this magazine coming out now I expect that we will get even busier. Jamie I think it is time we hired some extra help in sales," Mr. Smith said. "Congratulations Jamie…"

INFLUENCE syn. (Webster's new world dictionary)
Implies the power of person or things (whether or not exerted
consciously or overtly) To affect others [He owned his position
to influence]; **Authority** implies the power to command
acceptance, belief, obedience, etc., Based on strength of
character, expertness of knowledge, etc. [A statement made on
good authority]

Influence is one of the most powerful words in business.
Look at such people as Bill Gates, Donald Trump, Lee Iacocca
and other successful top executives who have framed the
world of business. One thing they all have in common is the
influence they possess through their words and actions, which
shows in how successful they have become. But influence in
business can also be devastating when it is served up with a
cup full of bitterness, deceit and retaliation. Remember earlier
in the book when I told you, that if a customer is pleased with
your service that they will tell five others of the experience, and
if they are dissatisfied with your service that they will twelve
others of their experience. Whether it is one customer or twelve
any loss of business can be devastating.

Many companies take referrals for granted. That's ok for
them because their customer base or product availability is
substantial, which we all know can eventually lead to disaster
when they become complacent.

It doesn't matter what your current standing in business is,
when you take referrals for granted: then you start taking your
customers for granted. This is where poor customer service is

born and rears its ugly head because to many companies only look at the here and now, and not the future.

But what about the smaller specialty shops, the commissioned sales person, or the one surviving on tips; they cannot afford any negative feedback. Restaurants and Deli's have the highest rate of failure of any small business; this according to banks and local Chambers of Commerce. The number one reason typically is undercapitalization. In many cases though; failure falls on lousy customer service. Here let me ask you this. What are the top three reasons that would keep you from going back to a restaurant, hair salon or car dealership? In no particular order they would probably be: price, selection and customer service. WOW! customer service is in the top three, that is because we all value good customer service. How many times have you sat in a restaurant with two or more people, and sometime during the conversation some has said. "the food here is great, but their service is lousy." Their service is lousy. That is just another way of saying I may not go back there again. Then a few days later a friend asks you to join them for lunch. You begin thinking of your choices. Instantly you cross off the place with lousy customer service. First one customer, then another and another, soon the sign appears in the window, SORRY WE'RE CLOSED.

Which customer will be the straw that brakes the camels back? Are you willing to take the risk and find out?

Influence can be the building blocks of success; a strong foundation to build our company on, or the acid that tears apart even the strongest of structures. Think of customer service as the stock market, you want your business to be like the bull market: everyone buying your product or service, customers seeking you out, telling their friends, family and co-workers to invest in your business. That is a true sign of success. To many times though businesses are like a bear market, customer service falters, customers (investors) start leaving, the value of your company dwindles until the strain of lost business forces you to shut down leaving your fellow employee's wondering, Why?

"Because the customer has **Influence,**
we have the hope of **More** customers."

Take the time, work with your staff or re-think how you can be a better customer service professional.

It was said that "A fool and his money are soon parted." You worked hard to get where you are at. Invested time and money, had great plans for success: do not lose it by forgetting the most important building block of business:
Your customers and the influence they have.
"Because the customer has **Influence,**
we have the hope of **More** customers."

When it comes to customer service, treat others the way you would want to be treated. I know, I know, you can never please every customer, but you can turn a difficult customer into a possible ally by referring them to someone else who you think might be able to help them. Remember Macy's from Miracle on 34th Street. Like you, I have a list of people that I would refer any difficult customer too if I could not help them. It is how you handle the referral that will dictate the kind of response. Telling a customer that they are a royal pain and a waste of your time will most likely result in the customer bad-mouthing you and your business. I suggest putting a picture of someone in your back room and after the customer leaves go back there and tell the picture what you think, this will help you to never cross the line in referring a bad customer to someone else.

Yelling at or degrading a customer never works in making a referral. Instead you could say; I am sorry that we could not work this out, you have an important issue that I could not resolve. I have called this business for you and explained the situation, they're looking forward to your call. If there is anything else I can do for you in the future, please give me a call, Thank you for your time.
Influence, which way do want the scale to tip, Fifty plus years of success, or going out of business.

"Because the customer has **Influence,**
we have the hope of **More** customers."

Chapter VIII.

Because of the customer, We Exist.

"I have a job to do"
Eric

When it comes to customer service there is one example that stands out above all the rest. Tipped employee's. People who rely on tips as a major part of their income will either make or break themselves when it comes to customer service. When ever I go out to a restaurant I am always looking to see how the entire staff responds to not only me, but to the other patrons also. This is why I have something special planed for you right now.

Are you ready for a task? Grab a pencil and paper, and write down what you expect the most from your favorite restaurant. Now put it aside until after your next visit.

We have all had a meal at a sit down restaurant and we know that sometimes they can get very busy. That's why the second part of your task takes place at your favorite restaurant during the busiest meals of the day, lunch or dinner. As you enter start making notes on your visit and keep making notes throughout the entire visit until you exit, when you get home find the sheet where you wrote down your expectations and compare notes. Do not be alarmed when your expectations were greater than your actual visit. Sadly this same experience happens with our own customers. Do they go home and compare notes? Do they expect more from us than we actually offer: or do we exceed their expectations?

Never be afraid to ask your customers for their feedback, and be ready for sometimes shocking results. If your customers feel that you care enough to listen to their concerns, it will make it much easier for them to except the times when we screw up. We all know that everyone is capable of making mistakes, how we handle it will set us apart from the rest of the pack. No company is perfect by any means, by accepting that we can and will make a mistake now and then and having a plan in place to rectify the situation before it spirals out of control simply doesn't work. Plans are great, actions are better.

Now I firmly believe that the customer is **NOT** always right, but knowing how to handle a charged situation is a true sign of a customer service professional. Remember…

"Because the customer has **SENSIBILITIES,**
We must be **CONSIDERATE.**"

That is why we must fully understand our customers needs, and put their needs first. Just because we put their needs first does not mean that the customer is always right. When we have a situation where no matter what we do or have done can not satisfy the customer, then we must politely point them in a different direction. Saving both you and the customer further conflict, and possibly ensuring that you will get future referrals.

But how do we compare the relationship that we have with the customers? It's simple. Let us use a mental picture.

Let us think of the company, customers and customer service relationship as a jet. The company is the body of the jet, the customers are the wings that give the company lift. The engines are customer service from which we draw our power. You're a brand new company ready to take off. Your flight plans are complete, your course is set and you are ready to go. You have made all the right decisions and preparations to this point. Just before your maiden flight you do one final pre-trip, your checklist is complete, all is well, LET'S GO!

Your company taxi's on to the runway turns and gets its final OK from the tower. You open your doors to a crowd of people and you can feel the power pushing you down the runway. Your customers are overwhelmingly happy, customer service is strong. Your company picks up speed until you lift off and take flight. As the success of your company grows, you fly higher and higher until one day when your company levels off. Profits are good, customer service is strong and the customers remain loyal. Then one day your company hits a critical point in its future, turbulence. Customer service starts to fail, you start losing sight of what lifted your company off the ground in the fist place, your customers and customer service. Suddenly the flight gets rough and you ignore the warning signs. You keep flying hoping the problems will go away, but they only intensify.

"Tower we're experiencing some turbulence, please advise."

"Flight, stockholders are happy, continue on course, trim the excess."

"Roger that tower, trimming excess customer service."

As you continue to trim customer service you start losing more and more customers causing un-do stress to your jet
Until you suddenly cry out.

"Tower MAYDAY, MAYDAY we have lost all engine power, the wings are becoming weak."

"Flight prepare for crash landing."

"Tower it's too late, we are headed for bankruptcy call my attorney."

This company, like many other companies crashed because they lost sight of the most basic principle in business: customer service. You can make all the right plans, have all of the best products and hire the most educated people around, but without customer service you too will crash.

Train, and re-train, your employee's to always do right by the customer. Remember when we all work for the customer, we benefit. When we fail the customer we all suffer the same fate. Let us not forget that everything we have or could ever want is simply, because of the customer and it all begins with customer service. Bottom line.

BECAUSE OF THE CUSTOMER, WE EXIST!

It has been twelve months since Eric's dismissal from Sternhaven Incorporated International and Jamie's rise to sales executive of the year, Eric has bounced from job to job trying to reclaim the glory he knew back in college: Jamie continued on her path of success, being named Wholesalers Trade Sales Executive of the year for 2003, 2004 & 2005.

Mr. Sternhaven filed bankruptcy in 2006 and closed his business for good, losing all concept of customer service which he once proudly demonstrated so many years before. While Mr. Smith vaulted his company to a customer service Mecca with the help of Jamie Easystreet, his new Vice President of Sales.

Eric's job outlook had not yet improved. He continued to move from job to job each time learning more and more about himself and why he had failed so poorly. He was quickly realizing that the lessons he received from Mr. Sternhaven had taken him nowhere. Eric finally came down to earth when he realized that it was his arrogance and out-spoken nature that had hindered him. After attending a sales seminar Eric landed a new job as a sales person for a local company. This time Eric would not have a fancy office, a company car or an extra large expense account. Instead just a simple desk in the back corner of and over crowded office, and a banner that hung on the wall behind his desk that reads,
Because of the Customer

Eric arrived promptly at 7:30 am and introduced himself to the receptionist.

"Good Morning, I'm Eric NoDeale and I start work here today."
"Good Morning Eric, I'm Sandi. From all of us here at Smith's Apparel Wholesalers, Inc., welcome aboard, let me show you to your desk."

Eric followed Sandi to the back corner of the office and a small desk.
"Here you go Eric," Sandi said. "This is your desk, the restroom and break room are down the hall. Oh! And you have an 8:00 am sales meeting in the break room."

"Thank you Sandi." Eric replied.

Eric sat at his desk for a moment surveying his new surroundings before going to his first sales meeting. As Eric arrived in the break room he was greeted by Mr. Smith.
"Good morning, Eric," Mr. Smith said. "Welcome aboard, are you all settled in?"

"Yes sir," Eric replied.

"Please Eric, call me Mr. Smith, when I hear sir I think I should be smoking a cigar."

"Ok Mr. Smith" Eric replied.

"We will be getting started as soon as my Vice President of Sales arrives, Oh, here she is now." Mr. Smith said.
"Good morning Jamie, I'd like you to meet Eric NoDeale our newest member of sales, Eric this is Jamie Easystreet."

"We have already met," Jamie said. "Eric and I graduated college together, how have you been Eric?" Jamie asked.

"Not as good as you Jamie," Eric replied. "But I am working on it. "Mr. Smith, Eric asked; I noticed you have many banners hanging around the office and also here in the break room that read, Because of the customer: Why?"

"Jamie, I think you should answer Eric's question." Mr. Smith said.

Jamie turned to Eric with confidence and said. "Eric, let me ask you a question, why are we in business?"

Eric thought for a moment then replied. "Because we have something, the customer needs."

"Yes!" Jamie said, because we have something the customer needs, which brings me to our first rule Eric." "Because the customer has a **NEED,** we have a **JOB** to do."

Eric smiled. "I like that, Eric said. I have a job to do."

Chapter IX.

It takes Teamwork.

"Everyone has the potential to be great..."
Frank Briggs

Together, **E**ndurance, **A**ttitude, **M**anage,
Willingness, **O**pen, **R**eality, **K**eep.

Eight words that mean Teamwork, Football players do it.
Hockey players do it. Baseball players do it: Teamwork.
Married couples, mountain climbers and successful companies also
do it: Teamwork. No matter what your job is or the position you
hold, everything we do involves teamwork. Have you ever had the
privilege of coaching any youth activity, baseball, soccer, basketball
or any other activity where you were calling the shots? I have, back
in 2002 when my son played baseball in the youth league. His
coach at the time did the coaching for the team only because his

own son was a player. This man, this so called team leader never cared about how the boy's did as long as his son was playing. After five games the coach's son up and quit the team, so did the coach the day before our next game. I received a call from the city's recreation dept. asking me if I would step in and take over. I agreed to only if the other parents would approve of me being the coach. To my surprise they told me that three of the parents had already called requesting me. Needles to say, I accepted graciously and took over a team who's current record was 0 wins, 4 loses, 1 tie.

The next night as we gathered at the field, I noticed that the players all seemed discouraged during our warm ups. Just before the game as I read the line-up off I told the boy's that I was very proud of them, and all that I expected of them was to do their very best: but mostly I wanted them just to have fun. As we took the field that night the coach from the other team walked over to me and said that I should just forfeit now and save the team a lot of embarrassment. I turned to the coach and asked, "Why?" He just laughed and walked away. Six innings later he was not laughing, but yelling at his team for losing to a bunch of boys he had underestimated, By a score ten – two. I told my team to go out on the field and just have fun. Even when they made a mistake I offered encouragement, but what was so amazing is how that simple gesture brought them together as a team. When the season was over I had taken a bunch of boy's from last place with 0 wins, 4 loses and 1 tie; to a fourth place finish with 10 wins, 7 loses, 1 tie.

Whether you are a self employed individual, working for a small business or part of a large corporation, you too need teamwork to be successful. Have you ever seen an automobile engine when it has been torn apart, how many parts there are? What happens when one of those parts stops working correctly? It's simple, the engines fails to run smoothly. It takes all of the parts to do their job working together. The same can be said for a company, that we must all work together for a smooth operation. Everyone counts on someone, somewhere to due their part in our everyday successes. We all play the part of coaches, players and spectators working together as we go throughout our daily routines.

I have put together from past experiences my own version of teamwork. I have used this several times with great results when we understand what teamwork is all about.
When it comes to teamwork, let us talk with one another, encourage each other with our words and actions. Where teamwork is the main focus, take the time to talk with others after issues arise, do not just put up posters that say a brief comment about teamwork. Take the time to explain them, because posters by themselves never really get to the point and can sometimes leave you guessing.

Think about the people you work with, can you do everything your business offers, and still meet the customers high expectations, probably not. That's because it takes a team of people to make it happen. Did Neil Armstrong get to the moon by himself? No, there were two other men in the spacecraft with him, but before they lifted off from earth there were literally thousands of workers who built, transported, checked and double checked every component, not to mention the round the clock staff of mission control. TEAMWORK, it took teamwork to make it all happen. Do not just say we work as a team, be a team, bask in the glory when it goes right, and share the blame when it falters.

Together: we can achieve.

When we work together, great things will happen. Success will be there for those willing to work hard to achieve the sometimes unimaginable. When Lee Iacocca took over the Chrysler Corporation years ago he coined a phrase that still holds true today. "In business you either lead, follow or get out of the way" Chrysler was on the verge of collapse and yet he called upon his employees to come together as a team. Success came to Chrysler many times over, but it took teamwork, real teamwork and people coming together.

When we talk about achieving great things, lets look at it a bit more simply, In 1953 Sir Edmund Hillary did what no other person had yet done, he stood on top of the world as he scaled the highest peak Mt. Everest. It had taken months if not years of training prior to this achievement, not to mention all of those who helped him along his path: and yet to this day most people cannot tell you the name of the man who scaled Mt. Everest with Sir Edmund Hillary, he was just a simple man, a Sherpa from Nepal named Tensing Norgay, and yet without his help, Sir Edmund Hillary would have been just another man looking up at the top of the mountain instead of standing there.

What mountains do you climb? And who is on your team that helps to get you there? Make sure your team is recognized: Together, we can achieve.

Endurance: For the long haul.

Pace yourself, take your time you were always told. We are in it for the long haul. Marathon runners, Tour De France riders, Iron man participants all have one thing in common, endurance. Watch sometime in person or on television when these competitions are taking place, look closely at the faces of the athletes: you will see pain, sacrifice, struggle and dedication. These athletes know what lies before them, and yet they push on against all odds, for they know only one quest, to finish. When you hear them speak of their training one word rings out loud and clear: Endurance. As we work together in business for the common good of the customer, we too need endurance to finish our quest, customer satisfaction. Pain, sacrifice, struggle and dedication, these words hold true in business also, as we come together as a team.

Success, is not a nine to five job: but the willingness to sacrifice a little extra time, going through the pain of commitment, struggling to meet deadlines and being dedicated enough to see it through.

What races are you running? What is your training like? Can you see the finish line of your quest? Is your team ready? Do you have what it takes to be a winner? Remember it takes endurance, to go the long haul.

Attitude: above all else.

Every one has the potential to be great, not everyone has the motivation. For every one leader there are ten followers waiting to be given instructions. What makes a sled dog racer chose which dog will lead the pack? Simply, the dog which shows the greatest ability: and which dog the pack understands to be the leader. Come on, even in our own human references we refer to the boss as the top dog, or the leader of the pack in a race. It is because as humans we must have someone we can look up to for guidance, unless we ourselves strive to be the top dog.

Everyone has the potential to be great: this is very true, some people fear what they do not understand and because of this they will take a lesser path and step in line behind the others. On the TV show M*A*S*H there was once a reference to what makes a hero. Alan Alda's character Hawkeye Pierce stated that it usually was someone who was tired, scared and confused with nothing else to lose: who became a hero. "I'm tired, scared and hungry" he said, "I have nothing else to lose." and with that confronted the situation.

What about the hero's in business? Who are they? Usually someone who is tired of watching bad things happen to the company by a lack of leadership, then stepping up to the plate they take control, make tough decisions and have the vision and tenacity to see it through.

In World War Two a young man from Texas still wet behind the ears was forced to grow up and be a man before his time. His father had left the family during the depression when things got tough. A few years later his mother died leaving him to be the man of the house. He dropped out of school at fifteen and worked two jobs to take care of his younger siblings. Audie Murphy at seventeen with the help of a neighbor decided to join the military. Branch after branch turned him down because of his size, until the army accepted him. While going through basic training Audie took every possible class to learn what he did not receive from school. He wanted more out of the military than most, he had: Attitude above all else, and the motivation to see it through. He treated his comrades just like his family, took a leadership role and did what he could to protect those around him. Audie Murphy became the most decorated war hero of WWII because he had the drive and ambition to do what was needed, when it was needed.

We all work with toxic individuals who, no matter what, complain about everything: but when the time comes to do something about it, they simply look the other way. In order to be truly successful, we MUST have a good attitude above all else. Get away from the negativity and work together for the common good of all. Everyone has the potential to be great, not everyone has the motivation.
Empower yourself to lead, inspire the uninspired and have, Attitude: above all else.

Manage: to hold true to Success.

Through an overwhelmingly tough situation, a flight crew is forced to Land a plane on the Hudson River, with hours and hours of training and calm communication, they managed to hold true to success of saving the passengers of that flight. The captain and crew were touted as hero's but humbly said they were only doing what they were trained to do. Still, hero's none the less: we will all for ever be thankful for their dedication.

How many times in business are you touted as a hero? Do you manage to hold true to success through unmanageable situations? Captain Sullenberger (Sully) who landed his plane on the Hudson River said: that it was endless hours of training which led to the way his crew handled that emergency. I cringe at the thought of what would have happened to that flight if the crew had just stopped training once they had their wings: and yet in business all too many times we stop training our staff once we have them comfortably in their positions, then wonder why our businesses collapse. Training cost money, some companies look at this as a needless expense until things start to go wrong, then wish they had done things differently.

"Be the ball", "Stay on target", two lines from two different movies, both of them referring to the same conclusion: success. In business we must hold true to success even when the odds are sometimes stacked against us. Training and communication are the key elements, like the events that took place on June 6th 1944. As the sun rose in the sky and the fog lifted over the English Channel, a plan which had been set in motion long before this date, was about to be unveiled in what to this day is still the greatest invasion by a combined military force. French, Canadian, English and Americans were among those who stormed the beaches, scaled the cliffs, landed gliders or parachuted into Normandy France on what is now known as the longest day. It did not matter what the color of your skin was, your ethnicity, or even what religion you were, everyone had a job to do and the vision to see it through. With bullets flying, bombs exploding and men dying, the troops pushed on. They had too, for the sake of all mankind. Their struggle and sacrifice was difficult but through it all they managed to hold true to success.

Our battles in business can not even come close to those of Normandy, and yet when things get tough we start blaming others for our own mistakes. I do not care how tough things get, we all need to buck up and face the daily challenges that face us. We must storm the beaches of adversity, fight through the hedgerows of complacency: We must continuously push ahead. We know where we want to go, know what path we should take to get there, and expect that sometimes it will be rough, but if we can manage to hold true to success, we too will be successful.

Willingness: to be Open minded.

Think of all the wonderful inventions, foods and electronic gadgets we enjoy: Now ask yourself. How did we start to enjoy them? Because someone, somewhere, somehow had the willingness to be open minded. Take an egg for instance, think of the person who looked at a chicken and said, "I think I will eat the first thing that comes out of it's backside." And yet today, eggs are one of our most common and enjoyed foods.

Ever since man has been in existence he has looked to the sky, often wondering what makes a bird take flight. As the centuries passed, man and bird lived together. Sometimes idolized, often hunted. But one question has always been on mans mind.
What makes a bird take flight and not me?
Great thinkers throughout the centuries pondered this very thought over and over again, until two very unsuspecting brothers from Ohio who owned a bicycle shop in Dayton: looked to the sky and wondered, "Why not?" Orville & Wilbur Wright were very successful at selling bikes: they also pondered the idea of building cars. Their thoughts however kept reaching for the sky. So once again they looked to the sky for their inspiration: and an idea was born. In order to fly, they realized it would take more than just a set of wings: it would take power, more power than man alone could ever generate.

With the help of Charlie Taylor, who worked for the Wright brothers at their bicycle shop, they develop a power source strong enough to give lift, but not to heavy as to weight down their flying machine. On the morning of December 17th 1903 at Kitty Hawk North Carolina, man achieved flight; for twelve seconds only, but it set the stage for man to reach even higher. Just five decades later, man would reach space: not himself yet, but the first object to successfully circle the Earth in space. Sputnik a Russian satellite not only caused a great fear during the Cold War era, but caused both American and Russian scientists to become more and more open minded. America and Russia went back and forth in the race to reach further into space, and on July 20th 1969 man set foot on the moon. The Wright brothers gave us the inspiration, the willingness to be open minded, believing that man could fly.

As we work for the common good of our own companies, how open minded are we? Are we set it our ways? Or, do we have the willingness to try new things. It frustrates me when ever I hear that "We have always done it like that."
Not every new idea is a good one, but we need to open our minds to the possibilities that there is something more: if we just let our minds dream.
If you want to reach the moon, you need to shoot for the stars, and beyond. Create your very own think tank at work, try new ideas, dare to dream, and have the
Willingness to be open minded.

Open: To explore new frontiers.

Most of us have gone hiking at sometime in our life. Did you stay on the beaten path? Or did you explore new frontiers. If we truly want to challenge ourselves we must move off the beaten path, take the road less traveled: let ourselves see what else lies before us. Take a chance.

In the early eighteen hundreds then President Thomas Jefferson commissioned one of the greatest explorations of a young American Nation. In May 1803, two canoes and one boat filled with men and supplies set forth on what would become a two year journey filled with peril and discovery. Meriwether Lewis, Secretary to the President and army officer William Clark were chosen to lead the "Corps of Discovery" exploration to the west to find a river route that would lead to the Pacific Ocean. Along the way Lewis and Clark met many challenges from native people who were not the friendliest, to some of the most unforgiving terrain. They faced near starvation and illness, and yet they pushed on facing each challenge with an open mind, overcoming adversity at each turn in the river and every cliff they climbed.

Have you ever noticed a young child learning what the world holds in store for them, they too will overcome adversity. They explore everything, taking chances because they have not yet learned about fear.
They're tenacious by nature, fearless by design.

Take a group of children between the age of three and five: put them in a large room with nothing but four chairs, two blankets and a plethora of foam building blocks in various shapes and sizes. At first the kids will all sit and stare each other, then one of them will instinctively start to place the blocks into some kind of structure. As they continue to build, others will fall in line and help. Keep watching as they build, when the structure falls, they simple clear the area and start to build again. Why? Because children will always explore new frontiers, new ideas until they get it right. This reminds me of something my grandfather told me years ago when I was young. That the difference between an optimist and a pessimist is: an optimist knows things will get better and a pessimist is sure that they won't. This is why we need to reach inside ourselves and find that inner child: when we lose the ability to be open minded, when we are not open to exploring new frontiers and new ideas, when we are fearful of taking that first step. A journey of a thousand miles begins with just one step forward, take that step.

Tenacity is the willingness to go on even when the odds are stacked against you and others fall short. When you face challenges at work, Are you tenacious? Do you over come adversity by clearing your road blocks and starting over? Or: do you simple fall in line afraid to explore new frontiers? Open your mind: and you will open new doors: doors to a new frontier, letting your positive outlook determine your positive outcome.

Reality: to do right by each other.

They say it takes a village to raise a child, everyone doing their
part for the greater good: hunters and gatherers, builders, cooks
and caregivers. Teamwork, Wow! What a concept, and yet it
has been going on since time began.
Early man realized that they needed each other to survive, that
they had to do right by each other in order to be successful,
their future depended on it. And yet today in business we
think we can do it all on our own: until things go wrong, then
we try to find anyone else to blame for our own short comings.
If it takes a village to raise a child, then do you not think that
it takes teamwork to make a business successful? Earlier in the
chapter we read that "together we can achieve." This is now
truer than ever when we have the reality to do right by each
other. Share not only your successes when things are positive
with those you work with, but those times when things go
wrong as well, do not point fingers at each other, this causes
stress and to much stress will bring down any structure.

After the Lewis and Clark Corp of Discovery exploration of
1803 opened up the wonders of the west, people of all kinds
would sacrifice everything to get their part of what this young
country offered. For some it would be land, others the riches
of gold in California and for some just a chance to make a new
beginning in a new land.

As the great push west escalated, so did the need for men to
step up and lead wagon trains of people, supplies and livestock
to their new futures beyond the Missouri River.

As thousands upon thousands moved west they put their futures in the hands of those trusted individuals they believed would deliver them safely to their destination.
Sickness, weather and the occasional confrontation from the local natives who we were unfamiliar with this newcomer would take a great toll: but as long as they worked together they would eventually make it to their new lives and new homes beyond the horizon out west.

When we fear the unknown, we let things cloud our judgment. In our path to do right by each other we sometimes do not take chances, causing us to lose sight that everyone is important. As we pushed west, we feared the local natives. We were told by a select few explorers that they were blood thirsty savages, but in reality they could have taught us so much about family, nature and the idea that it takes a village to raise a child. Instead we let our ignorance dictate their future.

As we work together to create teamwork, we can not let our ignorance dictate the outcome. We are all different, with different views. Let us learn from each other; taking what we can from each other and building something wonderful.
As long as we keep the Reality to do right by each other,
We will succeed.

Keep; moving forward to success.

As time passes, so do our accomplishments. I know that we have all had that dream in our lives of something different, something wonderful, something new; but did we ever take the next step to see it come to fruition. Probably not, we simply just passed it off to a dream and only a dream. Once again, fearing what we do not totally understand; never having the willingness to be open minded or open to exploring new frontiers.

As I pass through the years, looking at all the things we have to use and enjoy, I am reminded that all these things started as a dream of someone who kept the dream alive by moving forward to success. Walt Disney, creator of Disneyland dreamed of a place where the world could come together and be happy. Walt Disney once gave us this saying which is featured in the end credits from the movie, "Meet the Robinsons".
"Around here however, we don't look backwards for very long, we keep moving forward, opening up new doors and doing new things, because we are curious…and curiosity keeps leading us down new paths." Walt Disney, creator of the "happiest place on earth." Do you have a dream? Are you curious? Be like Walt Disney: keep your dreams alive; who knows what great things will come from your simple dream. Remember, everyone has the potential to be great, not everyone has the motivation.

A few years ago my wife and I came across a plaque that read, "Believe in your dreams and they may come true, believe in yourself, and they will." apropos words for us to live by. As we look forward to our future, let us not forget the past, for the past holds our dreams, and our aspirations.

To reach the moon, you must shoot for the stars: reaching higher and higher with every passing day.

When we work together: What mountains will we climb? Will we have the endurance to see it through? Will we have the attitude to make it happen? Can we manage to hold true in the tough times? Have the willingness to see outside of the box? Be open to taking that first step? Do we have the reality to know that it takes teamwork to make it happen? And the strength to keep going when the times get tough?

Together, we can achieve.
If we have the,
Endurance: for the long haul.
And have the,
Attitude: above all else.
And,
Manage to hold true to success.
While keeping the,
Willingness to be open minded.
And,
Open to exploring new frontiers.
All the while having the
Reality: to do right by each other.
And through thick and thin,
Keep moving forward to success.

Chapter X.

<u>The Speech That Started It All.</u>

"Because of the customer, We exist."
Frank Briggs

Many times in our lives inspiration happens from a simple gesture such as a smile, to seeing the Grand Canyon for the first time. Everyone has the potential to be great, not everyone has the motivation. For me: my inspiration and motivation all started when I joined my Toastmasters club in Coeur d' Alene Idaho. Like many other members, I was slowly persuaded to visit as a guest and decided to join.
Selling North Idaho Toastmasters (S.N.I.T.) was not a typical Toastmasters club, we not only held our regular meetings, but also held a book club where we read and study books on customer service and business itself.

Like America with its diverse cultures, Selling North Idaho Toastmasters is diverse with members from many different professions. We gather together for the common benefit of all, uplifting and inspiring each other through speeches, evaluations and table topics.

But, Toastmasters is not just about speeches, it also focuses on leadership skills. From the club level to the International Headquarters, Toastmasters builds stronger more confident leaders and speakers through their clubs. This is why so many companies are getting on board starting clubs so their employees too will benefit. Toastmasters Clubs are a safe place where friends and colleagues gather to share speeches and get constructive feedback while serving as club officers and filling other roles during the meetings that help their members grow both personally and professionally. It is here that I received my inspiration for this speech that ultimately led to me writing this book.

Here is the speech that started it all.
Because of the Customer

Because of the Customer

Are customers important?
YES THEY ARE.

Do we need customers?
YES…YES WE DO!!

Because the customer has a **NEED,**
we have a **JOB** to do.

I want you to think right now about where you work and what kind of business you offer. Go ahead take a moment.

Now I would like you all to take a minute and write down three other companies that also offer that same business.

If you know your market place well this should be quite easy. I can see by Looking around the room that some of you wrote down your answers quickly, while some of you struggled to form your list. Those who formed their lists quickly understand that their customers have a choice with whom they will do business with. Remember you are not the only game in town, the customer has choices.

Because the customer has a **CHOICE,**
we must be the **BETTER** choice.

This is why we must always know what our competition is doing: looking at ads in the newspapers, by listening to radio and television ads: keeping up with the market place. Lee Iacocca former CEO of the Chrysler Corporation once said "In business, you either: lead, follow or get out of the way" Be the better choice, be a leader. If you are not the lead dog then the view never changes.

Now when a customer comes to us, we know that the customer will have questions and concerns: apprehension and excitement. How we first approach the customer will set the tone: remember you don't have a second chance to make a first impression, Make it count.
Have you ever read the book "**Raving Fans**" by Ken Blanchard & Sheldon Bowles, in the book it says we need to understand the customers needs: and put their needs first.

Because the customer has **SENSIBILITIES,**
we must be **CONSIDERATE.**

Do not treat your customers like idiots. This is why we must take the time to fully understand our customers needs: and put their needs first.

But can anybody here tell me: How soon does the customer need us? Is it tomorrow, the next day, next week or RIGHT NOW?!... That's right, it is right now.

Because the customer has **URGENCY,**
we must be **QUICK.**

So when you tell a customer, I'll get right back to you. Either we call them right back and give them the answer they seek: OR, we communicate to them that we are still working on their concern, and as soon as we have more information we will be in contact with them. A little courtesy goes a long way. Treat others the way that you would like to be treated.

Look around the room: Is there anybody else just like you sitting here? No probably not. As I look around the room I see that you are all a little different from each other: just as each and every one of your customers are a little different from one another. Remember that each customer is different, each with their own special needs. This is why we must learn to move with the emotional tide and change our course for a successful customer journey.

Because the customer is **UNIQUE,**
we must be **FLEXIBLE.**

But what exactly does the customer expect from us?
Is it low expectations? **NO!** What does the customer expect from us? Is it medium expectations? **NO!** If it is not low expectations or medium expectations: Then what does the customer expect from us? IS IT HIGH EXPECTATIONS? **YES!!!** It is high expectations.

Because the customer has high **EXPECTATIONS,**
WE MUST **EXCEL!**

Just because the customer is only a mile off. Do we stop there? **NO!** This is when we go the extra mile. We take our foot off the cruise control of customer service and we accelerate ourselves to **Raving Fan** service. Remembering the Customers needs: and putting their needs first.

Steven K. Scott author of the book "Mentored by a Millionaire" refers to the vision and plan for success as a Porsche, not just any Porsche. But a super charged, high performance machine capable of accelerating us to our goal. In this case: our goal is ultimate customer service.
Do you have the ability to handle such a machine? Or are you headed down a road that will lead to a customer service disaster by not finding an appropriate customer gear?

Remember that the customer can make or break us.

But how bad can a customer destroy us? How much business can we lose when a customer becomes un-happy with us? Let us take a quick look at that statistic.
A happy well satisfied customer will tell five others of their experience; however. A dissatisfied or angry customer can not wait to tell at least twelve others of their experience. This is more than a two to one margin of negativity.

CAN WE AFFORD THIS? IS THIS ACCEPTABLE?

The answer is simple. **NO!** Whether it is one customer or twelve, it does not matter, any loss of business can be devastating. You know how a gossiper can destroy a positive work environment: your customers too can destroy a positive business when they become distraught.

Because the customer has **INFLUENCE,**
We have the hope of **MORE** customers.

We all know the importance of referrals to our success in business, we rely on our customers to pass our name on to someone else, make sure they pass it on positively.

So in closing, Let us remember.

Because the Customer has:

a **NEED**
a **CHOICE**
has **SENSIBILITIES**
and **URGENCY**
and is **UNIQUE**
who has high **EXPECTATIONS**

Because the Customer has **INFLUENCE**
We have the hope of **MORE** customers.

Because the Customer has a **NEED,**
WE! We have a **JOB** to do.

THE BOTTOM LINE LADIES AND GENTLEMEN:

BECAUSE OF THE CUSTOMER,

WE EXIST!

Now that you have had a chance to read my book you can see that customer service really is a simple concept that goes way back in our own up-bringing.
Treat others the way that you would like to be treated. I know that making money is very important for both companies and employee's alike, but if we lose sight of the very glue that holds it all together, the customer: then we may as well close our doors now and turn off the lights.

I also want you to think about the fact that customer service starts every day once your feet hit the floor. It starts first with us. Then spreads to those around us: family, friends and co-workers. Each and everyone of us can build a pyramid of success where we can reach the top by making sure our building blocks are solid, based on integrity: and the willingness to go above and beyond each and every time we are given an opportunity. You never have a second chance to make a first impression: so everyday stand in front of a mirror and look at yourself and ask this question.
Am I the kind of person I would do business with?

Good luck to each and every one of you customer service professionals, make each day a good one, make each customer service situation a positive one and you too will reap the benefits that await you all:

BECAUSE OF THE CUSTOMER

First of all I would like to thank you for taking the time to read my book. I hope that you feel the same way I do about customer service and that you will put these 7 simple rules to play in your daily routine. If you have any further questions for me or would like to schedule a time where I can come visit your company and share my passion on customer service with your staff: then please feel free to visit my website at

www.knarfcoconsulting.com
or e-mail me at
frank@knarfcoconsulting.com
or
frank.knarfco@gmail.com

You can even reach me by sending a written request to

Frank Briggs
Knarfco Consulting
1609 North Bill Street
Post Falls, ID. 83854
208/659-6770

Knarfco Consulting:
"Improving customer service through teamwork"

Other books that will inspire you to become a better person: better leader, better customer service professional.

I highly recommend reading:

"Mentored by a Millionaire"
Steven K. Scott
Published by: John Wiley & Sons, Inc.

"Raving Fans"
Ken Blanchard
Sheldon Bowles
Published by: William Morrow & Company, Inc.

"How I Raised Myself from Failure to Success in Selling"
Frank Bettger
Published by: Simon & Schuster

"How to Win Friends & Influence People"
Dale Carnegie
Published by: Simon & Schuster, Inc.